The Magic Honey Jar

A Jewish Tale For Rosh Hashanah

By Rachel Mintz

To Eliya, Oz, Lavi, Arad & Tomer
Which make me happy
every single day

Once upon a time

in a green valley between high peaked mountains, was a small village. In that village lived an old lady. She lived there for so long, no one remembered when she came and no one knew her real name. Everyone in the village called her Safta Hava.

Safta Hava's house was small and cozy surrounded by flourishing gardens. She was known to help everyone who came to seek her help.

No matter if it was an upset stomach, an injured knee or lost love. Safta Hava would listen, nod slowly and disappear into the wooden shed behind her house. There she whispered chants and then she showed up with a teaspoon filled with sweet stew, which always helped.

One day, the people of the village woke up and saw a sign in the village square:

"Dear villagers, I am looking for a young person to help me clean my house for Rosh Hashanah. I will pay whoever comes the sum of 1 penny per hour, Shanah-Tova!"

Signed - Safta Hava.

Rosh Hashanah was due soon, and housekeeping help was needed. Cleaning the house, taking care of the garden and shed, made Safta Hava very tired. Many days passed and no one came in search for the job.

A few days later Safta Hava heard brisk thuds on the garden path.

"Hello" said a small boy, "I came for the job."

"What is your name?" asked Safta Hava.

"I am Ozzi."

"Shouldn't you be at school now, Ozzi?"

"We have a school break for the holidays and I can help around if you want."

Since no one else came, he got the job.

Safta Hava showed Ozzi how to clean the house, how to take care of the garden and then took him to her secret shed. It was filled with pots and jars, near the wall was a creepy old cupboard.

"You must not enter this shed alone" she said.

"I won't" promised Ozzi.

The next day Ozzi was in the garden when he heard noise coming from the shed. He walked quietly and peeked through the keyhole. He saw Safta Hava saying out loud, "I would like an apple" and then she chanted some words:

-   Oh magic cupboard, fill my tummy with something yummy".

There was a small buff, and ruff, and a noise which sounded like a cough, and an apple fell off the top shelf, right unto her feet.

"WOW! That is amazing" Ozzi could not believe his own eyes! He turned away before Safta Hava would catch him spying through the keyhole.

Therefore he missed the whisper that she said right after:

-   "Oh magic cupboard, stop and rest, the one you gave me is the best".

The day after, was one day before Rosh Hashanah, Safta Hava told Ozzi she was going to another village to help a young woman find a suitable groom. Ozzi waited in the garden until Safta Hava was well out of sight. He then tiptoed to the shed, it was quiet and dusty.

He knew he promised not to enter it alone, but what could go wrong?
Since Rosh HaShanah arrived, and Ozzi loved dipping apples in honey, he said out loud "I would like some honey".

Ozzi waited and then remembered he had to say:

- Oh magic cupboard, fill my tummy with something yummy".

There was a small buff, and ruff, and a noise which sounded like a cough, and a honey jar appeared at the top shelf. Heavy and glowing with yummy sweet honey. Ozzi grabbed it and leaped out to fetch an apple.

He didn't get far when he heard a small buff, and ruff, and a noise which sounded like a cough, and **few more** honey jars appeared on the top shelf.

"Oh well, today we dip not only apples in honey, but also bread in honey and bless each for a sweet and successful year" he thought, a couple of honey jars would be perfect.

Ozzi was thrilled to have enough honey to bring home for the Rosh Hashanah meal.

He was out in the garden when he heard a rumble sound from the shed. He run back swung the door open and was amazed…

There was a small buff, and ruff, and a noise which sounded like a cough, **more and more** honey jars appeared on the top shelf and fell off. The floor was already covered with honey jars rolling from side to side. Some of them broke, and the sticky honey poured all over.

"Help! Help!" Ozzi shouted as he rushed from the shed, the magic cupboard kept huffing and puffing as more jars came rolling off the top shelf.

Soon the shed was covered with honey jars, then they burst out to the garden. His friends arrived, "do something!" "Make it stop!" they all shouted and called at him. But there was nothing he could do.
"Stop! Please stop!" he pleaded toward the magic cupboard, but the jars kept appearing at the top shelf and falling off.

Soon the honey jars rolled into the village streets. They rolled and tumbled and were everywhere. Some of them crashed on side curves, splashing honey onto doorsteps and people.

Ozzi ran between the jars, not knowing what to do. People came out from their houses watching their little village taken over by hundreds of golden honey jars.

This went on all afternoon!

The village between the mountains was drowned in sweet honey. People could not walk the streets, children could not play, dogs could not run. It was nearly Rosh Hashanah eve and the village was helpless.

Then from a side alley came Safta Hava, she understood what happened the moment she saw the honey jars rolling down the road.

"You promised not to go in there alone!" She shouted over to Ozzi.

Safta Hava rushed to her home, she nearly tripped over the jars which covered her front yard and hurried to the secret shed.

The cupboard was making noises, coughing and spitting honey jars.

Safta Hava leaned forward and whispered:

-   "Oh magic cupboard, stop and rest, the one you gave me is the best".

The last jar popped out and hit the floor, as silence fell upon the shed.

The village was saved.

When the honey rush settled down, everyone in the village was angry at Ozzi.
They wanted a harsh punishment for him.

"Throw him to jail" they said to the mayor.

Ozzi apologized and said "it's Rosh Hashanah, I only wanted some honey to
dip my apple into".

"No, don't throw him to jail," said Safta Hava, "since it IS Rosh Hashanah
today, I have an idea which will teach him a lesson." She turned to Ozzi and
said: "You will have to eat all this honey, until the very last drop of it.

Ozzi began eating honey from the jars. At first he dipped apples, then bread, then he was so full he only dipped his finger. Soon his friends and family joined to help him. The whole village was licking honey and dipping apples.

They kept licking and dipping until the very last jar in the village was licked clean. It was after all the sweetest Rosh Hashanah they could remember.

Shanah-Tovah!

The End

Check These Short Story Books For Kids

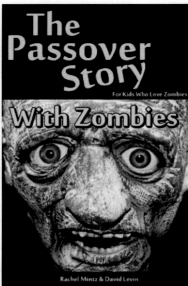

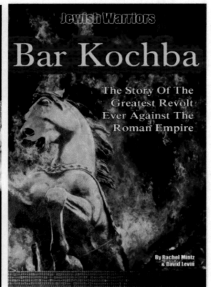

A boy deals with bullies at school like Judah Maccabee.	Passover exodus story with Zombies	The story of the legendary Bar Kochba.

Home, Sukkah, Classroom Quick Decoration Kit Books

Decorate your home or Sukkah with easy made book-kit! Create instant decorations and cut out colorful banners. Your home or classroom can be decorated in minutes.

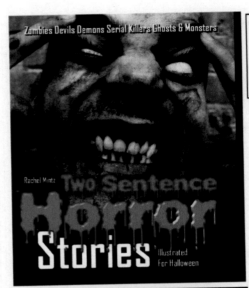

Not for sensitive people...
Two sentence horror stories
Morbid, disturbing Halloween book.

Children learn useful English proverbs with illustrated owls and pictures.

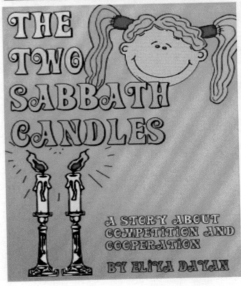

Written by a 10 years old girl, a delightful story about family, friendship and remorse.

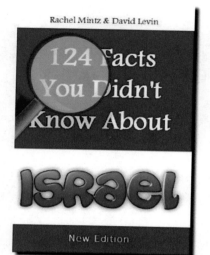

Fast, and exciting facts book about
Israel which will blow your mind!
124 amazing facts you didn't
know about Israel.

Think you know Israel?
Take the trivia quiz book about Israel...

Children activity books - Zooming out from extreme close-up images to identify the animal. With toddler rhymes about Piki The Flea.

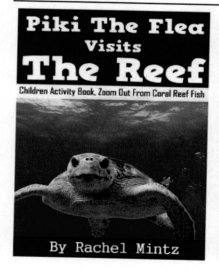

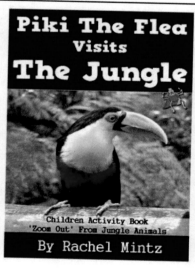

Order Jewish Festivals Fun Books

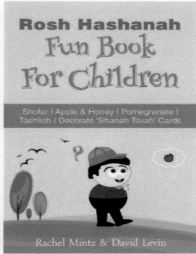

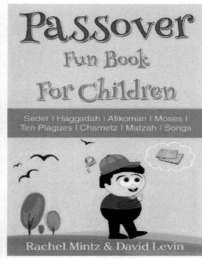

Fun way to enrich your kids about more Jewish festivals.

Learning the main themes and traditions for each festival with colorful puzzles and creative activities

Made in the USA
Middletown, DE
10 October 2016